Stress Management for the Healthy Type A
A Skills-Training Program

Stress Management for the Healthy Type A

A Skills-Training Program

Ethel Roskies

The Guilford Press
New York   London

© 1987 The Guilford Press
A Division of Guilford Publications, Inc.
200 Park Avenue South, New York, N.Y. 10003

Printed in the United States of America

Last digit is print number: 9   8   7   6   5   4   3   2   1

ISBN 0-89862-692-7

For my mother, Freda Sternthal Goldstein

Preface

The program you are beginning is designed to make good copers into even better ones. It is based on the premise that individuals like you are already competent in managing a host of occupational, family, and community responsibilities, but that this competence is achieved at too high a personal cost; indiscriminate and inefficient use of your abundant energy not only causes *unnecessary* psychological and physical distress, but also diminishes your effectiveness in reaching your goals. By improving your *awareness* and *control* of personal reactions, on the other hand, you can actually become more effective, achieving more at less cost. This program will show you how to do it, step by step.

   The program is divided into eight modules, each with its own rationale and specific homework assignments. The first serves as a general introduction, while the next three focus on basic skill building: increasing awareness and control of bodily reactions (physical stress responses), what you do (behavioral stress responses), and what you say to yourself (cognitive stress responses). The next two modules show you how to apply these skills to a variety of stress situations, both planning for predictable stressors and coping with unexpected stress emergencies. The final two modules are devoted, first, to increasing your stress resistance by developing strategies for obtaining needed rest and recuperation, and, second, to protecting your investment by learning ways of making stress management a lifelong habit.

   To change habits of long standing, particularly those which have generally served us well, is not an easy task. But you—the men and women likely to be exposed to this program—have gotten where you are precisely because you are able to confront challenge. This program facilitates your desire to learn new skills by making the process of change comprehensible, gradual, and rewarding. If you will accept the challenge of trying it, I think you will share the conclusion of many others who have preceded you: Learning to manage personal resources more effectively provides health protection for the future, but also makes the present more productive and more satisfying.

Ethel Roskies

Rationales

① Introduction:
Rationale for a program on stress management

What is stress?

Stress is a state that you experience when you are facing an important challenge (e.g., when you are making a presentation to your superiors) or threat (e.g., someone questions your competence) and there is a *possible imbalance between demands and resources.*

Stress arises, therefore, in a specific kind of *interaction* between you and environment:

1. You *perceive* a situation of *challenge, threat, or harm.*

2. You *consider* the outcome *important* to your welfare.

3. You *are uncertain* whether you *will be able* to successfully meet the challenge or avoid the threat.

Who experiences stress?

All of us inevitably encounter challenge or threat in the course of daily living, and in this sense stress is universal. What varies from individual to individual are:

1. The situations to which we are *exposed.* The potential triggers may be quite different for the junior executive compared to the company president.

2. The events *perceived* as stressful. Both past experiences (cultural and personal) and present circumstances (place, time, life situation, and mood) influence the way we evaluate situations.

3. The way stress is *experienced*—physical, emotional, cognitive, and behavioral signs.

4. The way we *cope* with it.

What produces stress?

Almost any event will trigger stress for somebody.

External stress triggers

Many stress triggers come from *outside:*

Unsatisfactory person–environment fit (responsibility without authority, job ambiguity, unpleasant colleague); change (new superior, new project, change in business conditions).

Or simply:

Daily hassles (the line at the bank, the car that won't start, the person who hogs the phone when you have to make an urgent call, etc., etc.).

Internal stress triggers

Some triggers come from *inside* ourselves (e.g., unrealistic self-expectations):

I can't afford to make a mistake.

I ought to be further in my job level than I am.

What happens during a stress episode?—A first look

Before	The trigger	Mobilization	Recuperation
Before the trigger: The mental and physical *set* with which you approach a potential stress trigger.	Traffic light, broken shoelace. New task to master. "That same old routine is getting me down." "Now that I'm 40, it's now or never." Change in job, family circumstances.	*Dealing with the trigger:* A state of war in which all resources—thoughts, feelings, and physical responses—focus on meeting the challenge or threat.	*After the battle:* Time for relaxation. Closure on what is passed. Energy replenishment. Ready for the next challenge or threat.

What happens during a stress episode?—
A second look

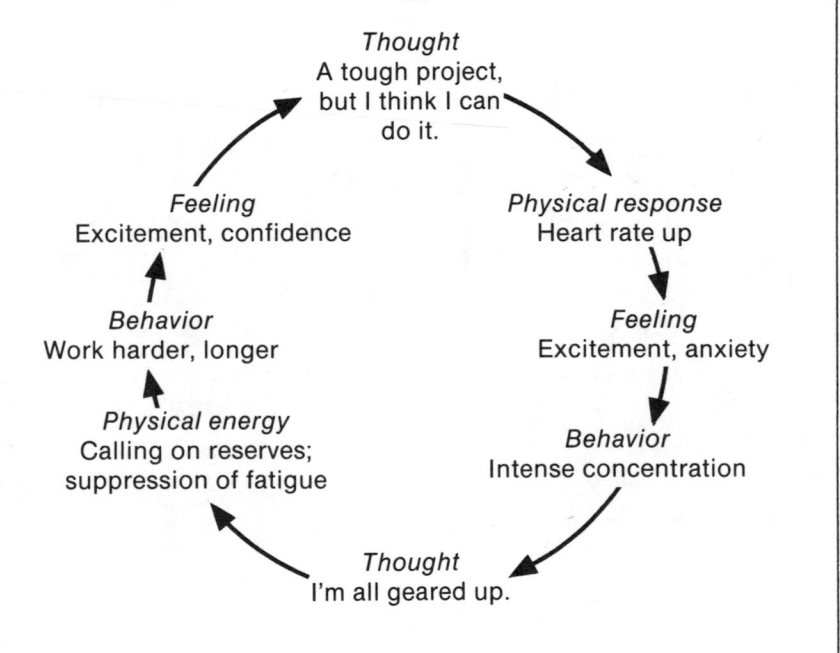

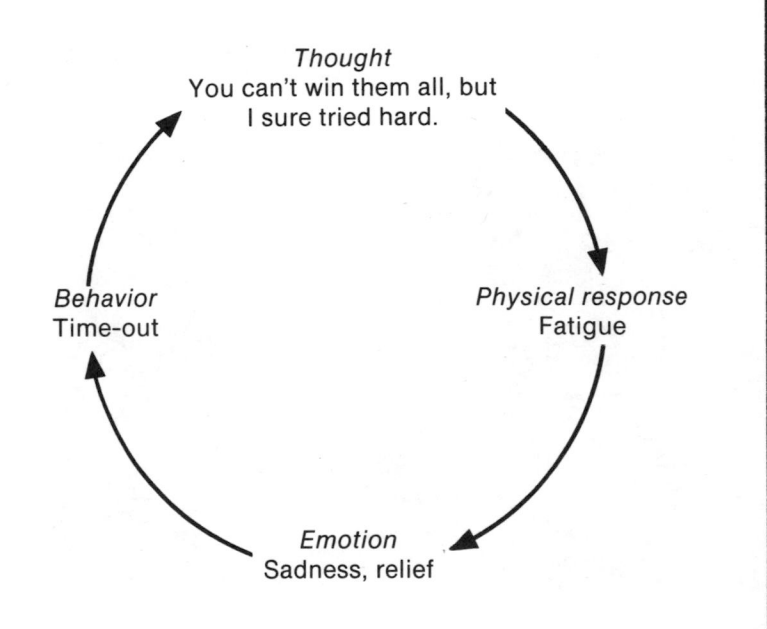

Mobilization

Recuperation

The "type A" response to stress

Before	The trigger	Mobilization	Recuperation
Before the trigger: Type A is highly vulnerable to threat/challenge because of his or her mental and physical set: a. Mental—expectations of self and others. b. Physical—constitutional hyperreactivity.	*Anything and everything:* Type A treats even minor obstacles as major provocations.	*All wars are nuclear wars!* Type A has no brakes to modulate the response. Therefore, arousal is too strong, too long lasting. Strong arousal may even interfere with performance.	*What's that?* Type A is unable to enjoy recuperation. He or she rests only when exhausted. No sooner is one battle over than the process begins again.

Why type A is ineffective

Too quick on the trigger.
Indiscriminately strong mobilization.
Too slow to recuperate.

Result: You get the job done, but with a too high, wasteful use of energy.

Goals
of this program:
"Effective use of energy"

1. *Learning* to be more *selective* in choosing *which triggers* to respond to.

2. *Learning to modulate* the *degree* of your response to any stress trigger.

3. *Minimizing* the duration of your mobilization.

4. *Maximizing* the benefits of your recuperation.

How are these goals achieved?

- By *learning to become more aware* of your physical tension level, your thoughts, and your behavior.

- By *learning skills to control* your physical tension level, your thoughts, and your behavior.

- By *practicing* these skills until they become a part of your life.

- By *using* these skills:

    In *preparing* for stressful situations.

    In *meeting* unexpected stresses.

- By *increasing* stress resistance:

    In *learning* to balance threat and challenge with pleasure and tension release breaks.

How is the program structured?

Learning new skills—whether the skill is playing tennis or stress management—takes time, effort, and practice. To facilitate learning in this program, we have made it a step-by-step process. There are eight modules;

1. *Introduction* to the program.

2. *Relax:* Learning to control physical stress responses.

3. *Control yourself:* Learning to control *behavioral* stress responses.

4. *Think productively:* Learning to control cognitive stress responses.

5. *Be prepared:* Learning to anticipate and *plan* for predictable stress situations.

6. *Cool it:* Learning *emergency braking* in unpredictable stress situations.

7. *Building stress resistance:* Learning to plan for rest and recuperation.

8. *Protect your investment:* Stress managements as a *lifelong investment.*

Format of program

When?

Where?

What happens if I miss a session?

What happens if I must be away for a whole week?

The first four modules are devoted to introducing the program and learning basic stress management skills: How to control *physical, behavioral,* and *mental* signs of stress.

In each case the format is the same:

A. *Self-awareness*—What do you have to *know about yourself* to institute change?

B. *Developing new skills*—What do you have to *do* to institute change?

C. *Applying new skills*—How do you *apply* the new skills to daily life?

Once you have learned the ABCs of stress management, the next two modules (5 and 6) are devoted to showing how to *combine* and *apply* them in order to play the stress management game.
This involves:

Learning how to *anticipate* and *plan for* potentially stressful situations.
Learning to maintain or regain your cool even in the face of *unexpected stress.*

Module 7 deals with increasing your general *resistance to stress.* The emphasis is on learning how to increase your stress tolerance by scheduling "pleasure breaks" into your daily routine.

The final module is devoted to *protecting your investment,* learning strategies that will make stress management a lifelong habit.

You can't always control the world *outside,* but you can learn *to control the way you respond to it.*

The importance of homework

No one has ever learned to play tennis or speak French simply by reading a book or listening to a lecture on the topic. Rather, the learning of a new skill takes repeated practice in real-life situations.

The same is true of stress management. To benefit from this program, it is important that you try out during the course of your daily routine what we talk about during a session. Only by trying something out, reporting on your experience at a subsequent session, and receiving corrective feedback, will these new skills truly become a part of you.

To systematize and guide this practice, we have developed a series of homework assignments. Everyone knows that homework is a drag and that trying to find time to do it only adds to your stress! We agree!

But homework is also essential for learning. We have kept the homework assignments:
- Short and snappy (no more than 20 minutes a day).
- Relevant to your daily routine.

Aren't you worth spending 20 minutes a day on yourself?

R-E-L-A-X

② Rationale for managing bodily tension

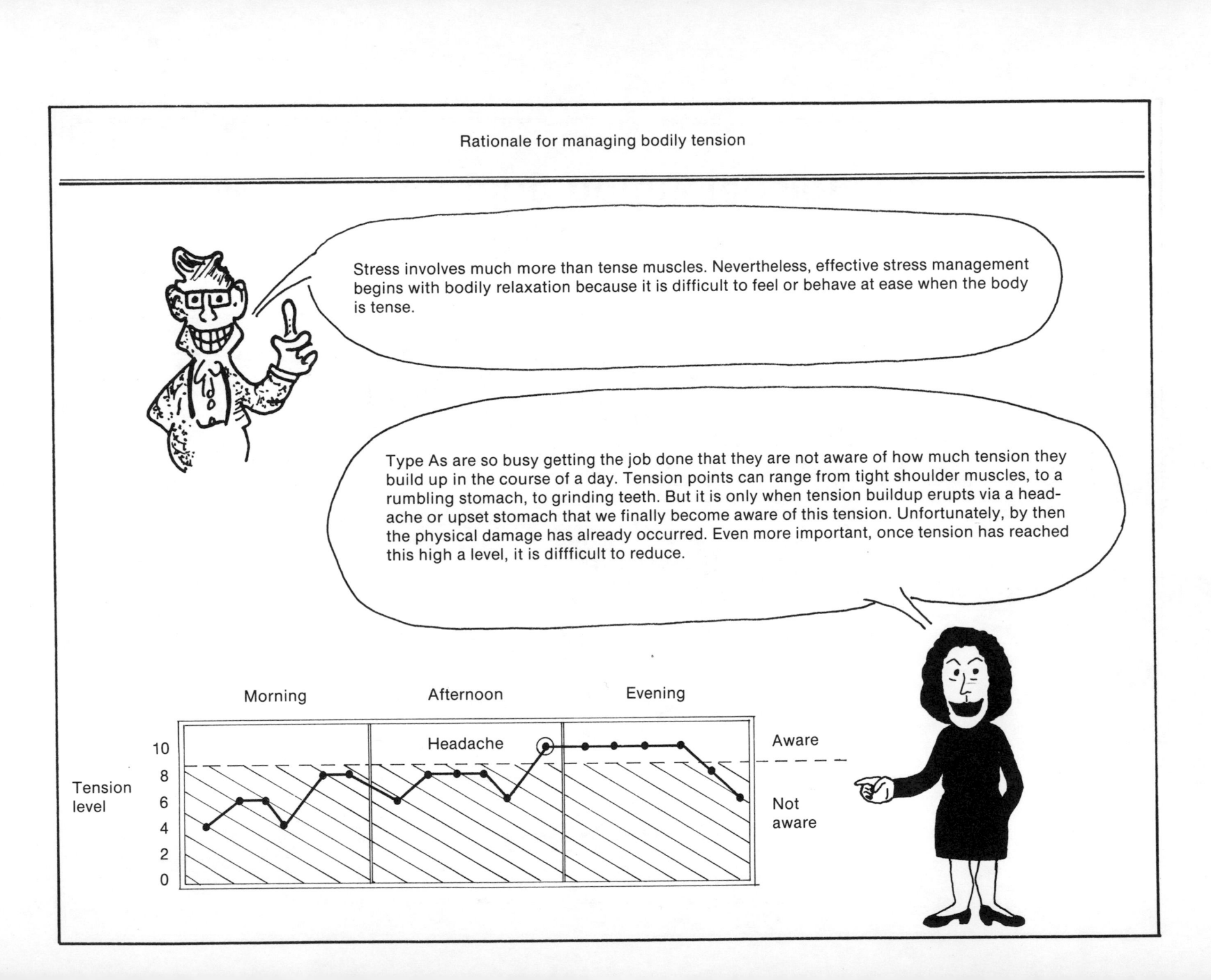

Steps involved in learning
to manage physical tension

Effective management of physical tension means keeping your bodily tension at a level that is *comfortable* for you and *appropriate* to the situation. To achieve this aim, a number of skills are required:

A. Awareness skills

● Of small variations in bodily tension.

● Of relationships between feeling states (e.g., anger) and bodily states (e.g., pounding heart).

● Of what constitutes a comfortable "cruising speed" for you.

B. Developing new skills

● Learning to discriminate a relaxed muscle from a tense one.

● Learning to lower overall body tension by relaxing muscle groups (e.g., forearm, jaw) one by one.

● Eventually, learning to use a single command to relax your whole body. Take a deep breath and R-E-L-A-X.

C. Applying new skills

● Once you have acquired the ability to relax upon command, this can be used:

● *To monitor and regulate tension during the course of the day:* By checking and reducing tension periodically (e.g., every time you pick up the phone), you can avoid harmful tension buildup.

● *To prepare for a potentially stressful situation* (e.g., an interview, a meeting): By doing so, you will have the advantage of entering the situation in a calm, collected manner.

● *To maintain or regain self-control during crisis:* When you are upset or overwhelmed, management of physical tension is the first step in achieving control over your reactions.

"Control yourself"

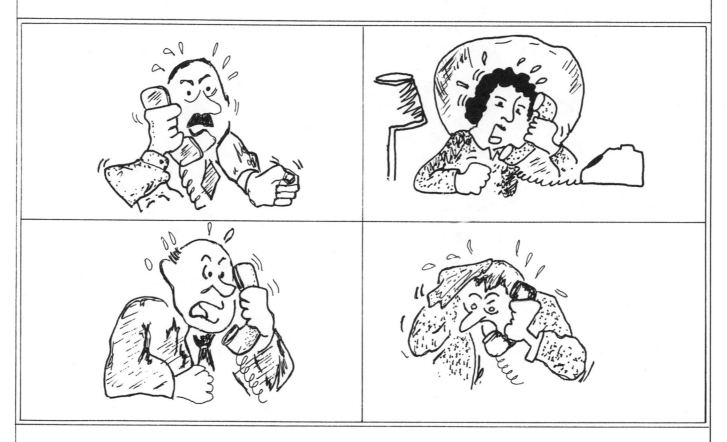

③ Rationale for
managing behavioral tension

Rationale for managing behavioral tension

When you are feeling overwhelmed by multiple demands and insufficient time, it may seem normal to speak curtly to your secretary, to tap your fingers impatiently during a meeting, and to bark into the interrupting telephone. Unfortunately, such displays of behavioral tension have a double negative effect:

1. The very act of raising your voice or pounding your fist increases the unpleasantness you are already experiencing, creating *within yourself* a negative spiral of escalating tension.

2. Behaving angrily or impatiently toward others leads them to respond in kind, creating *between people* a negative spiral of escalating tension.

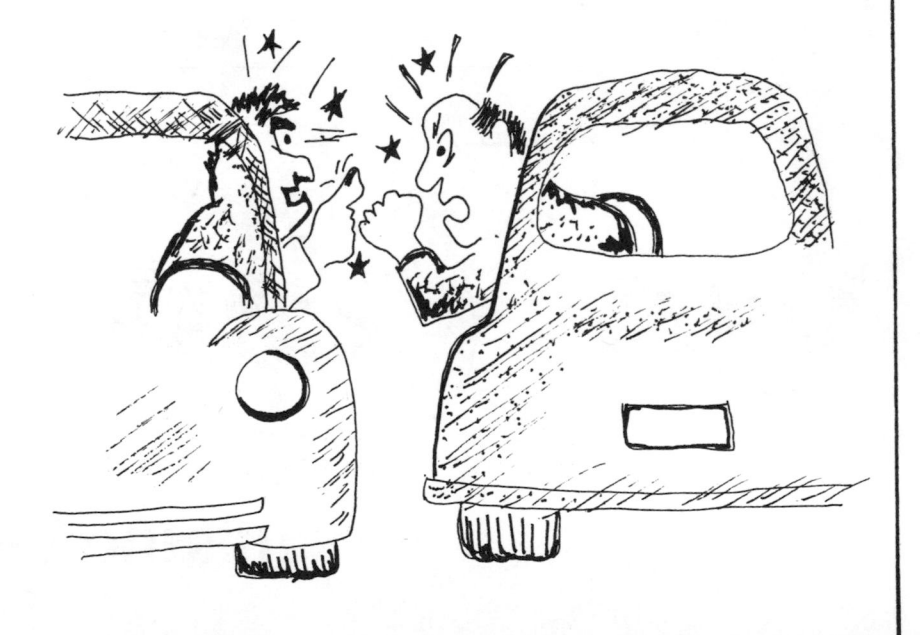

Many people believe that it is necessary to rant and rave when upset in order to "blow off steam." Unfortunately, by the time they have finished their eruption they have created such havoc—within themselves and in their relationship with others—that much time and energy is required to repair the situation. In contrast, the person who can manage his or her behavioral signs of tension expresses needs or complaints verbally, in a forceful but controlled manner. If not always master of the situation, he or she is at least in control of his or her *own behavior*.

Steps involved in learning to manage behavioral tension

Effective management of behavioral tension means that you can move quickly if necessary, express displeasure, and even assert your rights, *all without losing control*.

A.   Awareness skills

- Identify your personal signs of behavioral tension.

- Recognize the relationship between feeling state (e.g., frustration) and tense behavior (e.g., shouting).

- Recognize the situational and interpersonal triggers likely to provoke tense behavior.

B. Developing new skills

- Delay undesirable behavior.

- Engage in behaviors incompatible with the undesirable target behavior; for example, speak slowly to prevent shouting, attentively to prevent impatient tapping of fingers.

- Express needs and complaints verbally, in a nonhostile, controlled manner.

C. Applying new skills

- Express your needs or complaints in a controlled, appropriate fashion. Rather than bottling up anger or losing control, you can use anger purposefully.

- Increase desirable behaviors in the course of the day. The person who speaks in a calm, modulated voice, assumes a relaxed body position, and listens attentively will improve his or her interactions with others, as well as his or her own feelings of well-being.

- Use feelings of emotional upset as a yellow light, warning that special attention is required to monitor and regulate behavior.

Think productively

What a waste of time to be forced to sit here while others are getting ahead. In any case, I should already be at a higher level at my age. I wish Rodin had placed me in a running position.

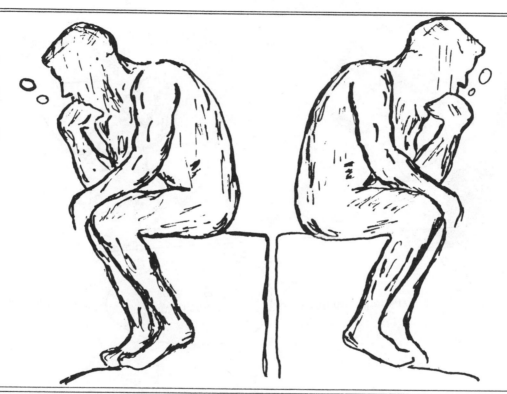

It's good of Rodin to let me sit and reflect for a moment. I would have liked to be at a higher level but given my age and background, I think I've done pretty well. There is also a lot of pleasure in my family and my friends.

④ **Rationale for managing self-talk**

All of us experience frustrations, disappointments, and defeats in the course of our professional and personal lives. How we interpret and react to them, however, depends very much on our individual "internal programs." Two people may be in the same situation of having a pet project turned down by a supervisor:

but if one says to himself or herself "Win some, lose some." while the other says "I can never get anything accepted."

then each is likely to feel very differently about himself or herself, the supervisor, and the desirability of trying again. External events provide the raw data of our experience, but it is our internal programs that determine how this experience is perceived and managed.

Many people are afraid that tinkering with thoughts is a form of brainwashing, leading us to react artificially.

On the contrary, more often it is our automatic thought patterns that interfere with our ability to judge each situation realistically and independently.

Learning to critically examine and modify our internal programs (self-talk) increases our ability to react more effectively and appropriately to the events we encounter. Productive thinking means the ability to use self-talk to *reduce,* rather than *increase,* your stress level.

Steps involved in learning to manage self-talk

A. Awareness skills

1. Learn to recognize unproductive self-talk, that is, self-talk that increases tension and discomfort.

A. Awareness skills (continued)

2. Critically examine the beliefs and habits that underlie negative self-talk.

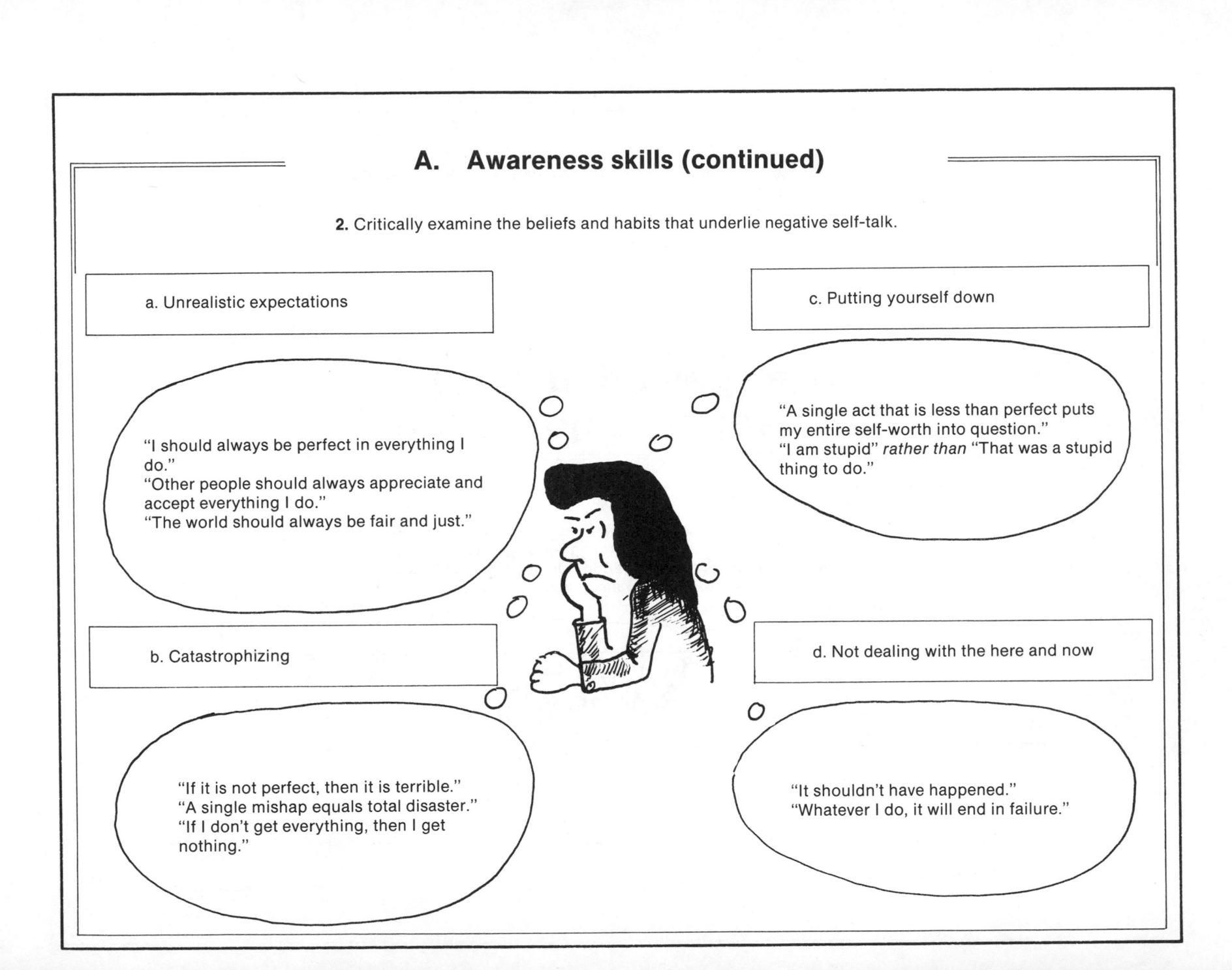

a. Unrealistic expectations

"I should always be perfect in everything I do."
"Other people should always appreciate and accept everything I do."
"The world should always be fair and just."

c. Putting yourself down

"A single act that is less than perfect puts my entire self-worth into question."
"I am stupid" *rather than* "That was a stupid thing to do."

b. Catastrophizing

"If it is not perfect, then it is terrible."
"A single mishap equals total disaster."
"If I don't get everything, then I get nothing."

d. Not dealing with the here and now

"It shouldn't have happened."
"Whatever I do, it will end in failure."

B. Developing new skills

Consciously replace unproductive self-talk with productive self-talk.

C. Applying new skills

Make self-talk work for you!

1. Develop habits of productive self-talk.

2. When you are upset, examine whether your self-talk is helpful or harmful. If it is harmful, change it.

When we think of stress, our usual tendency is to equate it with the unexpected and the sudden. But many of the stressful events in our lives result from *repeated reruns* of the *same situation* (e.g., the monthly project meeting with the hostile co-worker, the time pressure of striving to finish a report the day before deadline, the weekly lineup at the bank). By learning to recognize these chronic sore spots in our lives, we can also learn to take *effective preventive action* to avoid or reduce the stress involved.

Some people might be worried that learning to recognize and prepare for stress would take all the fun out of life. After all, is there not something unnatural in anticipating problems before they occur? But problems are part of life and they are going to happen whether you anticipate them or not. What trouble shooting does is to give you *better control* over problem situations because you are *prepared to meet them.*

Steps involved in learning to prepare for stress

Stress trouble shooting means learning to *identify* potentially stressful situations and to take *preventive action* that will either avoid the trouble spot or reduce its negative impact.

A.   Awareness skills

Identify

Identify situations that are *repeatedly* stressful for you. A good guide to the existence of a chronic stress situation is finding that your tension level *consistently* rises above the comfort zone in that situation, or with that person.

Become aware

Identify what specifically about the situation makes it stressful for you. Here it is important to avoid the booby trap of dwelling on the faulty behavior of someone else, and to focus instead on how this person affects you. After all, you may not be able to directly prevent a colleague from making hostile cracks during a meeting, or even your spouse from being persistently late in getting ready for a social gathering, but by pinpointing how this trigger affects *your* thoughts, *your* feelings, *your* behavior, and *your* physical functioning, you will be in a *better position* to take remedial action.

Specify goals

Specify what are the desirable and possible change goals: a changed situation, a changed reaction, or both.

B.   Developing new skills

1. *Planning (before)*   *Make an action* plan that will either (a) *prevent* the stressful situation from occurring (e.g., a well-planned schedule can avoid the time pressure of finishing reports at the last minute) or (b) *change your reactions* to it (e.g., "When a colleague starts making hostile remarks during meetings, I will take a deep breath, and then reply in a slow, calm voice, focusing solely on the business at hand"). Be specific: How will you modify self-talk, behavior, and physical reactions?

2. *Stay cool (during)*   In the heat of an ongoing stress episode, it is easy to feel overwhelmed and slip into old ways of doing things. But a moment's panic is not necessarily total disaster. *Stop.* Take a deep breath, and *start again.*

3. *Evaluate (after)*   *Review the stress episode* and your behavior during it. Make sure to *give yourself credit* for any positive changes in your own reactions, no matter how *small* and regardless of outcome. Changing long-standing habits is not easy, and success cannot be expected immediately. Moreover, even if you do not always master the situation, success in *controlling yourself* is a praiseworthy achievement in itself. After you have noted your progress compared to past performance, then *plan* for further improvements in future episodes.

C. Applying new skills

Begin small

- In learning to use stress planning skills, tackle one situation at a time. Maximize your chances for success by choosing a situation that is fairly simple and not too tension producing.

- Make a habit of scanning your weekly agenda to pinpoint stress situations that could be planned for.

- Whenever your tension level goes above the comfort level, use this as a signal to explore whether this stress could have been headed off by planning.

"A successful stress manager is an *effective stress planner.*"

Cool it

⑥ Rationale for learning emergency braking techniques

Rationale for learning emergency braking techniques

The phone rings. Your boss's secretary informs you that the boss wants to see you *immediately,* and the secretary's voice is less than cordial. . . .

You come home at the end of a long, hard day. Sitting in the driveway, *rusting in the rain, is the expensive bicycle* that your son *had* to have and that you haven't even paid for yet. . . .

You are driving along to work, feeling good in spite of the traffic. Suddenly, the oil gauge warning light flashes red. For the first few seconds, you ignore it, hoping it is just a momentary aberration. But the light remains stubbornly red. You start *thinking* of the inconvenience of having to take the car to the garage, the cost of a potentially expensive repair. . . .

All these situations are *stress triggers* that cannot be *antitcipated* and *planned for.* Instead, they are the *unexpected jokers* in the day's round of events, happenings that come out of the blue to *bedevil us.* It is unrealistic in this type of situation to try to *avoid anxiety/anger/ frustration completely.* Instead, the aim of a good braking system is to help us *maintain or regain self-control* in spite of our negative feelings. Once we are in control of ourselves, then we can decide how best to deal with the situation. Moreover, by focusing on achieving *self-control first,* we can avoid doing or saying things we are likely to regret later.

Steps involved in learning emergency braking techniques

Effective braking means learning to *maintain or regain self-control* when confronted by *unexpected stress.*

A.   Awareness skills

Applying the brakes: Each of us has personal signs telling us that we are *out of control* (e.g., flushed face, shouting voice). When these appear, it is important to have a signal telling yourself it is *time to brake.* This can be a simple *verbal command* ("Stop"), a *deep breath,* or a *visual image* such as a red light. Whatever signal you choose, *use it consistently.* It is your personal "code word" for making yourself aware that it is *time to brake.*

B.   Developing new skills

1. *Delay*
There are very *few stress situations* where you have to act *instantly.* If you are so upset that you cannot act in control, don't do or say anything for a few seconds. The *"time-out"* is a pause for you to focus on your primary objective: *self-control.*

B.   Developing new skills (continued)

2. *Incompatible behavior*
To counteract signs of disturbance, focus on behavior that is *incompatible* with the behavior you want *to avoid.* For instance, if you are so upset that your voice automatically rises to a shout, then focus on *speaking slowly.* Similarly, if your usual tendency when upset is to pace up and down, focus on *breathing deeply and slowly* as you do so. As you will soon discover, it is practically impossible to shout slowly, or to pace frenziedly while breathing deeply.

C.   Applying new skills

Proceed with caution
Once you feel in *control of yourself,* then you are ready to *deal* with the situation that triggered the disturbance initially. In some situations, you may need only a few minutes before proceeding. In others, a night's sleep or a day's reflection is desirable and possible before proceeding. In each case, however, the fact that you are in *control of yourself* will allow you to deal with the situation with greater *effectiveness and less strain.* Even more important, maintaining self-control allows you to *feel good about yourself* regardless of *outcome.*

Building stress resistance

"A pleasure a day keeps the stress AWAY."

⑦ **Rationale for learning to program pleasures**

Have you ever noticed that when you are feeling *particularly good about yourself* and the world, then the irritants of life do not bother you as much? On one of these good days you easily keep your cool even in the face of a subordinate's stupid error, or you respond with sympathy, rather than anger, to your teenager's poor mark in algebra. This does not mean that you are unaware of or indifferent to problems, but simply that your own feelings of *well-being* make you *more relaxed and more tolerant,* and hence better able to *cope* with the stresses of daily living.

The challenge is how to increase our *coping resilience* by making this feeling of well-being a *regular part of our lives,* rather than an occasional high. Obviously, physical well-being derived from adequate rest, sensible diet, and regular exercise is part of the answer. But even more important is the mental well-being gained from *pleasurable activities.*

Unfortunately, many of us feel that our lives are too crammed with work, chores, and obligations to allow time for pleasure regularly. We may have occasional daydreams about sailing the Greek Islands, really getting in shape, or pursuing an interest in music, but these are usually dismissed as unrealistic fantasies requiring too much time or money. In this way, pleasure is relegated to periodic "getting away from it all" or to some unspecified time somewhere in the future.

Not all pleasures, however, require *inordinate amounts of time and money.* A good dinner, a conversation with a friend, or even a moment's pause to appreciate a job well done can all be sources of pleasure. Even our daydreams can often be realized in part, if not completely. A private yacht and 6 months to sail the Greek Islands may be only a dream for the future, but sailing lessons at the local Y is a present possibility. Like savings, however, pleasures are unlikely to happen if we relegate them to time left over. Instead, a good resource manager *must budget for pleasure* in the same way that he or she *plans for other activities.*

Steps involved in learning to plan for pleasure

Effective planning for pleasure means learning to *build pleasures into your daily routine.*

A. Scanning possibilities

- Conduct a *brainstorming* session. Sit down for a half hour and list all the activities that have been or might be pleasurable for you. List *everything* you can think of, without stopping to evaluate.

- Observe yourself over the course of a few days. *Note those activities* that make you feel particularly *relaxed, satisfied,* or *replenished.*

B. Choosing an activity

- *Evaluate* each one of the activities you have listed in terms of costs (time, money, special equipment) and benefits.

- *Choose one* activity to begin with. Don't get hung up in searching forever for the "perfect" activity. Alternately, don't undertake too many activities at once.

C. Getting started

- *Develop an action plan.* Specify when, where, with whom, and how you will carry out this activity. Trouble-shoot by identifying possible obstacles and how you can overcome them.

- *Maximize* chance of success by setting realistic goals and arranging circumstances to facilitate reaching them. Enlist the support of your family and friends if this will help.

- *Reward yourself* for any change accomplished. In any new activity, even a potentially pleasurable one, beginnings are hard. Give yourself credit for these first steps.

D.   Keeping on

- *Reevaluate regularly.* At regular intervals take an inventory of your pleasurable activities. Is it time to add to the list or to change activities? There is nothing wrong with changing your mind. The criterion is *your* sense of well-being.

- Regularly *monitor* your pleasure level, just as you do your tension level. When your pleasure level drops below the comfort zone, take remedial action.

- During periods of high stress, *pay special attention* to your pleasure level. Even if some reduction is necessary, attempt to maintain at least a minimum level.

- Immediately after a high stress period, allow *extra pleasure time* for rest and replenishment.

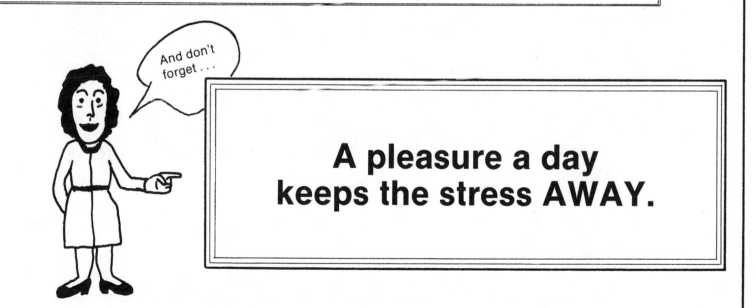

Stress management

⑧ Rationale for considering stress management as a lifelong objective

Anyone who has participated in this course has *invested* considerable *time* and *effort* in learning how to manage stress more effectively. You do not have to be reminded of what it took to attend two meetings weekly, practice homework daily, and fill out endless forms. . . . But you stuck to it and for most of you the benefits are obvious. Not only do you *personally feel better,* but in many cases spouses, co-workers, and acquaintances are beginning to *comment favorably* on changes in your behavior. You are now ready to graduate.

Graduation from a course, however, does not in itself guarantee a lifetime of effective stress management. Old harmful habits have *a much longer history* than do your newly developed coping skills, and it is very easy to slip back into old ways. Mark Twain once remarked that it is very easy to stop smoking; in fact, he had done it many times! Learning a new habit is relatively easy; to maintain it is much harder.

Fortunately, there are techniques that you can use to *protect your investment* in good stress management and even make it grow.

Anticipate

The best time to correct slipups is before they happen. To help you *anticipate* potential trouble spots:

- *Make a list* of the events or situations (travel, illness, job crisis) that might cause you to stop using your new stress management skills. Any disruption of the normal routine of life is a *signal* to pay careful attention to your *stress management strategies.*

- *Keep a chart of daily tension and pleasure levels.* A drop in pleasure level and/or a rise in tension level is a *signal* that you are *vulnerable* to stress problems. Try to correct the *imbalance* as soon as you can, either by lowering the tension level or by raising the pleasure level. If no immediate change in either is possible, be aware that you are depleting resistance resources and allow for a period of recovery after the crisis has passed.

Diagnose

- Sometimes, what has gone wrong may be fairly obvious to you. For instance, the announcement of a new boss for your department may create a situation of uncertainty with feelings of physical and mental tension. If the stress trigger is fairly obvious, then turn your attention to dealing with your reactions to it.

- Sometimes, you just don't feel right, but you can't put *your finger on any specific trigger.* Here is a chance to display your *talents as a sleuth.* Start keeping a *stress diary* again, noting hourly: situation, tension level, and signs. Once you have a week's records, sit down and study them. *What times of day, what situations,* and what *signs* correlated with high tension levels? *Read* the stress manual and see if you can pick up any hints as to where the problem lies.

Take remedial action

Once you have a tentative *diagnosis,* make a plan for dealing with the problem. During the course of this program you have learned a variety of techniques for controlling *physical, behavioral,* and *cognitive* signs of tension, as well as how to increase your pleasure level. Reread the manual and decide how to select and combine strategies so as to develop an *action plan appropriate to* the problem.

Reevaluate

After you have engaged in trouble shooting for a while, *reevaluate.* Has your remedial action improved your *tension–pleasure balance?* Are there any other strategies you might use to improve it still further?

Take credit

- Even constant practice of stress management will not make you *completely* immune to *all the vicissitudes of life.* But if you can keep your head when all about you are losing theirs, if you can learn to roll with the punches, then you will have done a great deal *to improve the quality of your life* and of the lives of people who live and work with you.

- For this, you have *reason to be proud.* You may not be able to *control the world,* but you have learned *to control yourself.*

Homework

Homework ①

Stress diary—Skills for detecting stress

What is the goal?

To *learn* to discriminate your physical and emotional signs of tension.

What do I have to do?

1. Fill in the sheet hourly, noting your tension level (low–moderate–high) and physical and emotional signs of tension. (See example sheet.)

2. Use a separate sheet for each day of recording.

Name: Example sheet   **Date:**

Situation | Tension level | Tension signs

Situation	Time	Tension level	Physical	Emotional
		Low — Moderate — High		
Woke up	a.m. 7h:00	Low	alert, ready to go	well-being
Arguing with son	8h:00	High	knot in stomach	anger, frustration
Working on new project	9h:00	Moderate	All systems go	interest, challenge
Phone call – financial data not ready	10h:00	High	heart rate up	irritation
Working on project	11h:00	Moderate	shoulder muscles tense	concentration
First draft finished	12h:00	Low	tired, hungry	satisfied
Lunch with project gang	p.m. 13h:00	Low	relaxed	friendly
Late for staff meeting	14h:00	High	running	hurry
Boring meeting	15h:00	Low	sleepy	boredom
Meeting real waste of time	16h:00	High	tense shoulder muscles	impatience
Desk work	17h:00	Moderate	concentration	resignation
Driving home	18h:00	Low	winding down	anticipation
Good dinner	evening 19h:00	Low	comfortable, relaxed	satisfied
Discussion with son re argument	20h:00	Moderate	apprehensive, tight	frustration
Discussion with wife re son	21h:00	High	stomach getting upset	anger, guilt
Beer — watch ball game	22h:00	Moderate	calming down	enjoyment
Ready for bed	23h:00	Low	tired, little tense	worried
	24h:00			

Name: **Date:**

Situation   Tension level   Tension signs

	Time	Low	Moderate	High	**Physical**	**Emotional**

Time

Low   Moderate   High

a.m. 7h:00
8h:00
9h:00
10h:00
11h:00
12h:00

p.m. 13h:00
14h:00
15h:00
16h:00
17h:00
18h:00

evening 19h:00
20h:00
21h:00
22h:00
23h:00
24h:00

Physical   **Emotional**

Name: **Date:**

Situation		Tension level				Tension signs	
	Time					**Physical**	**Emotional**
		Low	Moderate	High			

Situation	Time	Tension level	Physical	Emotional
_____	a.m. 7h:00		_____	_____
_____	8h:00		_____	_____
_____	9h:00		_____	_____
_____	10h:00		_____	_____
_____	11h:00		_____	_____
_____	12h:00		_____	_____
_____	p.m. 13h:00		_____	_____
_____	14h:00		_____	_____
_____	15h:00		_____	_____
_____	16h:00		_____	_____
_____	17h:00		_____	_____
_____	18h:00		_____	_____
_____	evening 19h:00		_____	_____
_____	20h:00		_____	_____
_____	21h:00		_____	_____
_____	22h:00		_____	_____
_____	23h:00		_____	_____
_____	24h:00		_____	_____

Name: **Date:**

Situation

Tension level

Time

Tension signs

Physical   Emotional

Time	Low	Moderate	High
a.m. 7h:00			
8h:00			
9h:00			
10h:00			
11h:00			
12h:00			
p.m. 13h:00			
14h:00			
15h:00			
16h:00			
17h:00			
18h:00			
evening 19h:00			
20h:00			
21h:00			
22h:00			
23h:00			
24h:00			

Homework ②

Improving self-awareness + RELAXATION

What is the goal?

To *improve* your ability to discriminate variations in physical and emotional signs of tension.

To *learn* how to relax muscles.

What do I have to do?

1. Fill in stress diary daily, as before.

2. Practice relaxation twice daily, noting tension level before and after each practice. (See example sheet.)

Name: **Date:**

Situation

Tension level

Tension signs

Time

	Low	Moderate	High

Physical   **Emotional**

a.m. 7h:00

8h:00

9h:00

10h:00

11h:00

12h:00

p.m. 13h:00

14h:00

15h:00

16h:00

17h:00

18h:00

evening 19h:00

20h:00

21h:00

22h:00

23h:00

24h:00

Name: **Date:**

Situation	Tension level		Tension signs	
	Time	Low Moderate High	**Physical**	**Emotional**

	Time	Low	Moderate	High
	a.m. 7h:00			
	8h:00			
	9h:00			
	10h:00			
	11h:00			
	12h:00			
	p.m. 13h:00			
	14h:00			
	15h:00			
	16h:00			
	17h:00			
	18h:00			
	evening 19h:00			
	20h:00			
	21h:00			
	22h:00			
	23h:00			
	24h:00			

Name: **Date:**

Situation	Tension level	Tension signs	
	Time	Physical	Emotional

	Low	Moderate	High		

Time

a.m. 7h:00
8h:00
9h:00
10h:00
11h:00
12h:00

p.m. 13h:00
14h:00
15h:00
16h:00
17h:00
18h:00

evening 19h:00
20h:00
21h:00
22h:00
23h:00
24h:00

Relaxation practice

Name: Example sheet

Date	Time		Tension level Before Low — Moderate — High	Tension level After Low — Moderate — High	Comments
April 13	First practice	8:30 am	High (✓)	Moderate (✓)	
	Second practice	9:45 pm	Moderate (✓)	Low (✓)	Difficulty relaxing shoulders
April 14	First practice	6:45 am	Low (✓)	Low (✓)	
	Second practice	7:30 pm	High (✓)	Moderate (✓)	Slept better
April 15	First practice	6:30 am	Low (✓)	Low (✓)	
	Second practice				
	First practice				
	Second practice				
	First practice				
	Second practice				

Relaxation practice

Name:

Date		Time	Tension level Before	After	Comments
	First practice				
	Second practice				
			Low　Moderate　High	Low　Moderate　High	
	First practice				
	Second practice				
			Low　Moderate　High	Low　Moderate　High	
	First practice				
	Second practice				
			Low　Moderate　High	Low　Moderate　High	
	First practice				
	Second practice				
			Low　Moderate　High	Low　Moderate　High	
	First practice				
	Second practice				

Homework ③

RELAXATION + Behavioral stress awareness

What is the goal?

To *improve* your skill in relaxation.

To *improve* your skill in discriminating *physical* and *emotional* signs of stress.

To *learn* to discriminate your *behavioral* signs of stress.

What do I have to do?

1. Practice relaxation twice daily, noting your tension level before and after each practice.

2. Fill in stress diary, adding your behavioral signs. (See example sheet.)

Name: Example sheet   **Date:**

Situation	Time	Low	Moderate	High	Emotional & physical	Behavioral
Traveling to work – bus slow	a.m. 7h:00		✓		impatience	keep looking at watch
Stress management session	8h:00			✓	interest, apprehension	alert, watch for cue
Correspondence	9h:00	✓			tense shoulders	
Planning session	10h:00			✓		voice rises
Site visit – trouble shooting	11h:00			✓	anger, irritation	walk and talk fast
Lunch	12h:00	✓			relaxed	gobbles food
Office meeting	p.m. 13h:00	✓			none – ordinary meeting	
Coffee break	14h:00	✓				laugh
Office meeting	15h:00				back to business	sit up straight
Answering memos	16h:00		✓		concentration	tap pencil
Squash game	17h:00			✓	effort, competitiveness	play to win
Traveling home	18h:00	✓			tired, relaxed	
Homework with child	evening 19h:00			✓	irritation	edge in voice
Dinner party	20h:00			✓	boredom	drinking too much
Dinner party	21h:00			✓	anger	parties = headache
Time to go home	22h:00			✓	anger	put on coat
Relaxation exercise	23h:00		✓		calming down	relax muscles
	24h:00					

Name: **Date:**

Situation	Tension level	Tension signs

Situation

Tension level

Time

	Low	Moderate	High

Tension signs

Emotional & physical	Behavioral

Time	Low	Moderate	High
a.m. 7h:00			
8h:00			
9h:00			
10h:00			
11h:00			
12h:00			
p.m. 13h:00			
14h:00			
15h:00			
16h:00			
17h:00			
18h:00			
evening 19h:00			
20h:00			
21h:00			
22h:00			
23h:00			
24h:00			

Name: **Date:**

Situation	Tension level			Tension signs	
	Time	Low Moderate High		**Emotional & physical**	**Behavioral**

Time	Low	Moderate	High
a.m. 7h:00			
8h:00			
9h:00			
10h:00			
11h:00			
12h:00			
p.m. 13h:00			
14h:00			
15h:00			
16h:00			
17h:00			
18h:00			
evening 19h:00			
20h:00			
21h:00			
22h:00			
23h:00			
24h:00			

Name: **Date:**

Situation	Tension level			Tension signs	
	Time	Low Moderate High		**Emotional & physical**	**Behavioral**
	a.m. 7h:00				
	8h:00				
	9h:00				
	10h:00				
	11h:00				
	12h:00				
	p.m. 13h:00				
	14h:00				
	15h:00				
	16h:00				
	17h:00				
	18h:00				
	evening 19h:00				
	20h:00				
	21h:00				
	22h:00				
	23h:00				
	24h:00				

Relaxation practice

Name:

Date	Time		Tension level Before	Tension level After	Comments
	First practice				
	Second practice				
			Low Moderate High	Low Moderate High	
	First practice				
	Second practice				
			Low Moderate High	Low Moderate High	
	First practice				
	Second practice				
			Low Moderate High	Low Moderate High	
	First practice				
	Second practice				
			Low Moderate High	Low Moderate High	
	First practice				
	Second practice				

Homework  4

RELAXATION + Modifying
behavior in one specific situation

What is the goal?

To *improve* your skill in relaxation.

To learn skills for *changing* tense behavior.

What do I have to do?

1. Practice relaxation twice daily, noting tension level before and after each practice.

2. Behavior change
   Step 1: Choose one specific behavior as a change target.
   Step 2: Choose one specific situation in which to implement change.
   Step 3: Prepare strategies for changing the target behavior the next time it occurs.
   Step 4: After the event, evaluate your actions and your feelings.
      (See example sheet.)

Name: Example sheet | **Date:**

---

1. Choose one specific *behavior* to change.

My target behavior is: Whenever I get upset, I start to shout.

---

2. Choose one specific situation in which you want to modify your target behavior.

Target situation:

When: Every week, starting next Friday.

Where: Project meeting

With whom: Joe, Bill, and Dave

---

3. *Prepare* a strategy for modifying your target behavior.

Incompatible behavior: As soon as I feel my voice rising, I am going to speak as slowly as possible.

Delayed behavior: If I shout, I will not say anything else for the next 60 seconds.

---

4. *Record* outcome.

What happened? I started to shout 3 times during meeting. Once I blocked it completely, the other 2 times it didn't last quite as long as usual.

How do you feel? Well, it's a beginning. Pretty good.

Name: **Date:**

1. Choose one specific *behavior* to change.

My target behavior is:

2. Choose one specific situation in which you want to modify your target behavior.

Target situation:

    When:

    Where:

    With whom:

3. *Prepare* a strategy for modifying your target behavior.

Incompatible behavior:

Delayed behavior:

4. *Record* outcome.

What happened?

How do you feel?

Name: **Date:**

1. Choose one specific *behavior* to change.

> My target behavior is:

2. Choose one specific situation in which you want to modify your target behavior.

> Target situation:
>
>   When:
>
>   Where:
>
>   With whom:

3. *Prepare* a strategy for modifying your target behavior.

> Incompatible behavior:
>
> Delayed behavior:

4. *Record* outcome.

> What happened?
>
> How do you feel?

Name: **Date:**

1. Choose one specific *behavior* to change.

My target behavior is:

2. Choose one specific situation in which you want to modify your target behavior.

Target situation:

    When:

    Where:

    With whom:

3. *Prepare* a strategy for modifying your target behavior.

Incompatible behavior:

Delayed behavior:

4. *Record* outcome.

What happened?

How do you feel?

Relaxation practice

Name:

Date		Time	Tension level Before	After	Comments
	First practice				
	Second practice				
			Low Moderate High	Low Moderate High	
	First practice				
	Second practice				
			Low Moderate High	Low Moderate High	
	First practice				
	Second practice				
			Low Moderate High	Low Moderate High	
	First practice				
	Second practice				
			Low Moderate High	Low Moderate High	
	First practice				
	Second practice				

Homework ⑤

RELAXATION + Modifying
behavior in several situations

What is the goal?

To *improve* your skills in relaxation.

To learn to *generalize* your behavior change skills to a variety of situations.

What do I have to do?

1. Practice relaxation twice daily, noting tension level before and after each practice)

2. Each time you become aware of tense behavior, introduce strategies to change behavior. Record the tension level and situation associated with the tense behavior, as well as the new behavior. (See example sheet.)

Name: Example sheet   **Date:**

Situation	Tension level			Tense behavior	New behavior
	Low	Moderate	High		
Anxious to get going		X		Rushed into office	Made a point to smile and say hello to co-workers
Interrupted during presentation			X	Shouted	Spoke more softly
Going to lunch	X			Rushed along street	Concentrated on observing faces of passers-by
Tense meeting			X	Fidgeting in chair	Took deep breaths.
Argument with son		X		Raised voice	Took 10-second time-out

Name: **Date:**

Situation	Tension level	Tense behavior	New behavior
	Low Moderate High		

Name: **Date:**

Situation	Tension level	Tense behavior	New behavior
	Low Moderate High		

Name: **Date:**

Situation	Tension level			Tense behavior	New behavior
	Low	Moderate	High		

Relaxation practice

Name:

Date	Time		Tension level Before	Tension level After	Comments
	First practice				
	Second practice				
			Low Moderate High	Low Moderate High	
	First practice				
	Second practice				
			Low Moderate High	Low Moderate High	
	First practice				
	Second practice				
			Low Moderate High	Low Moderate High	
	First practice				
	Second practice				
			Low Moderate High	Low Moderate High	
	First practice				
	Second practice				

Homework ⑥

RELAXATION + Modifying time-hurry behavior

What is the goal?

To *improve* your skills in relaxation.

To *apply* your skills in behavior change to changing "hurry sickness."

What do I have to do?

1. Practice relaxation twice daily, noting your tension level before and after each practice.

2. Every time you feel hurried, note the situation and your type A reactions. Then change your reactions, noting new behavior. (See example sheet.)

Name: Example sheet   **Date:**

Time-hurry level

No hurry	Moderate	Very hurried	Situation	Type A behavior	New behavior
		X	Driver in front too slow	Honk horn	Switch on radio and practice relaxation.
	X		Interrupted by co-worker while busy	Shuffle papers and wait for him to go	Tell him pleasantly that I am busy; make appointment for later.
	X		Eating lunch	Gulping food	Put down fork between mouthfuls.
		X	Co-worker speaks slowly during meeting	Tap foot and wait for chance to interrupt.	Concentrate on what he is saying
X			It's 4 pm and too many items left on agenda	Speed up; try to work faster	Decide to concentrate on most important

Name: **Date:**

Time-hurry level

No hurry	Moderate	Very hurried	Situation	Type A behavior	New behavior

Name: **Date:**

Time-hurry level

No hurry	Moderate	Very hurried

Situation	Type A behavior	New behavior

Name: **Date:**

Time-hurry level	Situation	Type A behavior	New behavior
No hurry Moderate Very hurried			

Relaxation practice

Name:

Date	Time	Tension level Before	Tension level After	Comments
	First practice			
	Second practice			
		Low Moderate High	Low Moderate High	
	First practice			
	Second practice			
		Low Moderate High	Low Moderate High	
	First practice			
	Second practice			
		Low Moderate High	Low Moderate High	
	First practice			
	Second practice			
		Low Moderate High	Low Moderate High	
	First practice			
	Second practice			

Homework (7)

RELAXATION + Self-talk awareness

What is the goal?

To learn to *improve* your skills in relaxation.

To learn to *become aware of* what you say to yourself when you are experiencing tension.

What do I have to do?

1. Practice relaxation twice daily, noting your tension level before and after each practice.

2. Every time you feel stressed, note tension level, situation, emotion, and self-talk. (See example sheet.)

Name: Example sheet   **Date:**

Situation	Tension level			Emotion	Self-talk
	Low	Moderate	High		
a.m.					
Bob heckles me during weekly project meeting			X	Anger, frustration	I'll never get it right enough to satisfy him.
p.m.					
Incompetent waiter at lunch		X		Impatience, anger	Damn it! I shouldn't have to pay for no service.
Colleague asks me questions I can't answer			X	Discomfort, embarrassment	He must think I'm an idiot.
evening					
Wife complains that I don't pull my weight at home			X	Self-pity, depression	She shouldn't put pressure on me now!

Name: Example sheet

Date:

Situation	Tension level			Emotion	Self-talk
	Low	Moderate	High		

a.m.

p.m.

evening

Name: Example sheet   **Date:**

Situation

Tension level

Emotion

Self-talk

Low   Moderate   High

a.m.
_____

_____

_____

_____

_____

p.m.
_____

_____

_____

_____

evening
_____

_____

_____

_____

_____

Name: Example sheet   **Date:**

Situation	Tension level			Emotion	Self-talk
	Low	Moderate	High		

a.m.

p.m.

evening

Relaxation practice

Name:

Date	Time		Tension level Before	Tension level After	Comments
	First practice				
	Second practice				
			Low Moderate High	Low Moderate High	
	First practice				
	Second practice				
			Low Moderate High	Low Moderate High	
	First practice				
	Second practice				
			Low Moderate High	Low Moderate High	
	First practice				
	Second practice				
			Low Moderate High	Low Moderate High	
	First practice				
	Second practice				

Homework ⑧

RELAXATION + Changing nonproductive self-talk

What is the goal?

To *improve* your relaxation skills.

To learn to *change* nonproductive self-talk into productive self-talk.

What do I have to do?

1. Practice relaxation twice daily, noting your tension level before and after each practice.

2. Each time you feel stressed, note tension level, situation, emotion, and self-talk. Then change self-talk and note change in emotion. (See example sheet.)

Name: Example sheet					Date:	

		Initial reaction		Modified reaction	
Situation	**Tension level**	**Emotion**	**Non-productive self-talk**	**New self-talk**	**Emotion**

a.m.

Low   Moderate   High

Situation	Tension level	Emotion	Non-productive self-talk	New self-talk	Emotion
Unsuccessful project meeting	X (High)	Despair	This meeting is a disaster.	This meeting not as good as I would like.	Disappointment

p.m.

| Boss turns down project | X (Moderate) | Frustration Defeat | I never win with him! | Well, this sales talk didn't work. I wonder what would. | Disappointment Determination |

evening

| Argument with son | X (Moderate) | Anger | He doesn't know how to be grateful! | I wonder what is eating him. | Curiosity |

Name: _____   **Date:** _____

Situation	Tension level	Initial reaction		Modified reaction	
		Emotion	Non-productive self-talk	New self-talk	Emotion
	a.m. Low Moderate High				
_____ _____ _____		_____ _____	_____ _____	_____ _____	_____ _____
_____ _____		_____ _____	_____ _____	_____ _____	_____ _____
p.m.					
_____ _____		_____ _____	_____ _____	_____ _____	_____ _____
_____ _____		_____ _____	_____ _____	_____ _____	_____ _____
evening					
_____ _____		_____ _____	_____ _____	_____ _____	_____ _____
_____ _____		_____ _____	_____ _____	_____ _____	_____ _____

Name:				Date:	

Situation	Tension level	Initial reaction		Modified reaction	
		Emotion	Non-productive self-talk	New self-talk	Emotion
	a.m. Low Moderate High				
	p.m.				
	evening				

Name:			Date:	

		Initial reaction		Modified reaction	
Situation	Tension level	Emotion	Non-productive self-talk	New self-talk	Emotion

a.m.

Low   Moderate   High

p.m.

evening

Relaxation practice

Name:

Date	Time		Tension level Before	After	Comments
	First practice				
	Second practice				
			Low Moderate High	Low Moderate High	
	First practice				
	Second practice				
			Low Moderate High	Low Moderate High	
	First practice				
	Second practice				
			Low Moderate High	Low Moderate High	
	First practice				
	Second practice				
			Low Moderate High	Low Moderate High	
	First practice				
	Second practice				

Homework (9)

SHORT RELAXATION + Combining
change in self-talk and behavior

What is the goal?

> To *learn a quicker* relaxation procedure.
>
> To *learn* to reduce stress by *combining changes* in self-talk and behavior.

What do I have to do?

> **1.** Practice side B of the relaxation tape twice daily, noting tension before and after.
>
> **2.** Every time you feel tense, note your nonproductive self-talk and your behavior, then try to reduce stress by changing both. Note new self-talk and behavior. (See example sheet.)

Name: Example sheet　　　　　　　　　　　　　　**Date:**

Situation	Tension level	Initial reaction		Modified reaction	
		Stressed behavior	**Non-productive self-talk**	**New self-talk**	**New behavior**
Spilled coffee on shirt during breakfast	a.m.　Low　Moderate　High　[X at High]	Clench teeth, swear.	What an idiot! I can't do anything right.	Well, nobody's perfect. How can I remedy this?	Change shirt.
Went to pick up urgent report and found secretary hadn't typed it	p.m.　[X at Moderate]	Boiling inside. Voice becomes loud and fast.	How inconsiderate! She never cares about my work.	I wonder how quickly I can get this typed.	Ask secretary to type this immediately.
Long line at supermarket	evening　[X at Moderate/High]	Mutter, glare at clerk.	Stupid store. They take our money and don't give service.	I don't like it, but there isn't too much I can do about it.	Amuse myself by observing others.

Name:			Date:		
		Initial reaction		**Modified reaction**	
Situation	**Tension level**	**Stressed behavior**	**Non-productive self-talk**	**New self-talk**	**New behavior**

Tension level

a.m.

Low   Moderate   High

p.m.

evening

Name:							Date:	

Situation	Tension level	Initial reaction		Modified reaction	
		Stressed behavior	Non-productive self-talk	New self-talk	New behavior

a.m.

Low   Moderate   High

p.m.

evening

Name:				Date:	
		Initial reaction		**Modified reaction**	
Situation	**Tension level**	**Stressed behavior**	**Non-productive self-talk**	**New self-talk**	**New behavior**
	a.m. Low Moderate High				
	p.m.				
	evening				

Relaxation practice

Name:

Date	Time		Tension level Before	Tension level After	Comments
	First practice				
	Second practice				
			Low　Moderate　High	Low　Moderate　High	
	First practice				
	Second practice				
			Low　Moderate　High	Low　Moderate　High	
	First practice				
	Second practice				
			Low　Moderate　High	Low　Moderate　High	
	First practice				
	Second practice				
			Low　Moderate　High	Low　Moderate　High	
	First practice				
	Second practice				

Homework  ⑩

RELAXATION + Awareness
of stress triggers

What is the goal?

To *improve skills* in relaxation.

To learn to *identify situations* that are repeatedly stressful for you.

What do I have to do?

1. Practice the short relaxation exercise twice daily, noting tension before and after each practice.

2. Every time your tension level rises above your cruising speed, note the stress trigger and classify it as "predictable" or "nonpredictable." (See example sheet.)

Name: Example sheet					Date:		

Tension level

Low	Cruising speed	High	Stress trigger		Predictable		Non-predictable
		X	Weekly project meeting		X		
		X	Line up at bank		X		
		X	Phone call from boss				X
		X	Traffic jam driving home		X		
		X	Repair bill for furnace				X

Name:			Date:	

Tension level

Low	Cruising speed	High

Stress trigger

Predictable

Non-predictable

Name:				Date:		

Tension level

Low	Cruising speed	High	Stress trigger	Predictable		Non-predictable

Name:		Date:	

Tension level

Low	Cruising speed	High

Stress trigger

Predictable

Non-predictable

Relaxation practice

Name:

Date	Time		Tension level		Comments
			Before	**After**	
	First practice				
	Second practice		Low Moderate High	Low Moderate High	
	First practice				
	Second practice		Low Moderate High	Low Moderate High	
	First practice				
	Second practice		Low Moderate High	Low Moderate High	
	First practice				
	Second practice		Low Moderate High	Low Moderate High	
	First practice				
	Second practice				

Ranking of stress triggers

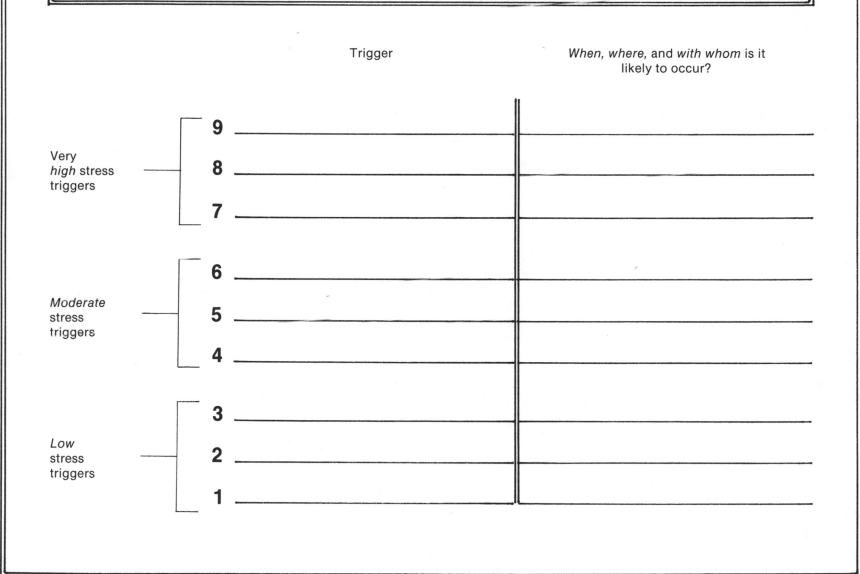

Trigger

When, where, and *with whom* is it likely to occur?

Very *high* stress triggers
9
8
7

Moderate stress triggers
6
5
4

Low stress triggers
3
2
1

Homework ⑪

RELAXATION + Preparing one specific stress situation

What is the goal?

To *improve* skill in relaxation.

To *learn* to prepare for one predictable stress situation.

What do I have to do?

1. Practice short relaxation twice daily, noting tension before and after each practice.

2. Choose one predictable stress situation in the moderate category each day. Plan a coping strategy, detailing what you can do before, during, and after the situation to reduce stress. Afterward, evaluate the effects. (See example sheet.)

Daily stress planner

Name: Example sheet   **Date:**

Plan
Self-talk strategy

Target situation	Before	During	After
Waiting in the doctor's office.	I know I'll have to wait, so I'll bring something with me to read.	If I start to get upset, remember she's not doing it on purpose.	Even if I don't succeed in staying completely calm, every little bit of progress counts.

Evaluation

What happened?	How did you feel?
Nothing out of the ordinary. Doctor kept me waiting as usual.	I felt pretty good because this time I didn't get upset enough to spoil my whole afternoon.

Daily stress planner

Name: **Date:**

Plan
Self-talk strategy

Target situation	Before	During	After

Evaluation

What happened?	How did you feel?

Daily stress planner

Name: **Date:**

Plan
Self-talk strategy

Target situation	Before	During	After

Evaluation

What happened?	How did you feel?

Daily stress planner

Name: Date:

Plan
Self-talk strategy

Target situation	Before	During	After

Evaluation

What happened?	How did you feel?

Relaxation practice

Name:

Date		Time	Tension level Before	Tension level After	Comments
	First practice				
	Second practice		Low Moderate High	Low Moderate High	
	First practice				
	Second practice		Low Moderate High	Low Moderate High	
	First practice				
	Second practice		Low Moderate High	Low Moderate High	
	First practice				
	Second practice		Low Moderate High	Low Moderate High	
	First practice				
	Second practice				

Homework  12

RELAXATION + Applying stress preparation skills

What is the goal?

To *improve* skill in relaxation.

To learn to apply stress preparation skills to a variety of situations.

What do I have to do?

1. Practice short relaxation twice daily, noting tension before and after each practice.

2. Every day, consult your list of stress triggers and plan a coping strategy for each one that is likely to occur. At the end of the day, evaluate the effects. (See example sheet.)

Name: Example sheet   **Date:**

| Anticipated stress triggers | Coping plan | | | Evaluation of effects |
	Before	During	After	
a.m. Traffic driving to work.	Prepare by leaving house in good time and in relaxed frame of mind (practice relaxation, eat breakfast).	If I start getting upset, Remember: "Stewing won't get me there any faster and I'll only be upset all morning."	After the drive, allow myself 5 mins. to unwind before starting workday.	I can't control the traffic, but I can control its negative impact on me. Bravo!
p.m. Explaining project to colleagues.	There are always some objections.	Don't jump! Listen to objections, then respond slowly.	A tough meeting deserves a good lunch!	
Secretary gives me messages as I'm ready to leave.	Ask her for messages 1 hr. before			It worked!
evening Discussion with daughter re failing mark in math.	Don't rake up all her sins. Concentrate on the problem at hand. Listen to her point of view.	If I get exasperated and shout, STOP, then try again.	After the discussion, try to talk about something pleasant. Mix some good with the bad.	A teenager is not easy, but at least I stayed in control of myself.

Name:				Date:
Anticipated stress triggers	**Coping plan**			**Evaluation of effects**
	Before	**During**	**After**	
a.m.				
p.m.				
evening				

Name:				Date:
Anticipated stress triggers	**Coping plan**			**Evaluation of effects**
	Before	**During**	**After**	
a.m.				
p.m.				
evening				

Name:				Date:

Anticipated stress triggers	Coping plan			Evaluation of effects
	Before	During	After	
a.m.				
p.m.				
evening				

Relaxation practice

Name:

Date	Time		Tension level		Comments
			Before	**After**	
	First practice				
	Second practice				
			Low Moderate High	Low Moderate High	
	First practice				
	Second practice				
			Low Moderate High	Low Moderate High	
	First practice				
	Second practice				
			Low Moderate High	Low Moderate High	
	First practice				
	Second practice				
			Low Moderate High	Low Moderate High	
	First practice				
	Second practice				

Homework  13

ONE-STEP RELAXATION + Coping
skills for stress emergencies

What is the goal?

To learn one-step relaxation.

To learn to deal effectively with *stress emergencies.*

What do I have to do?

1. Practice one-step relaxation regularly.

2. Everytime you feel signs of rising stress, use an emergency braking signal and institute strategies for regaining self-control. Then note the situation in which you used your emergency braking signal. (See example sheet.)

Name: Example sheet   **Date:**

Target situation

1. Boss criticizes work — I did the best I could.

2. I get carried away in argument; start to shout.

Signs of a rising stress	Braking signal	Strategies for regaining self-control
1. Tightness in chest and thought, "Boy, I'll never satisfy him!"	1. Say "stop."	1. Take deep breath and physically relax chest muscles.
2. Raised voice.	2. Visualize red light.	2. Stop speaking for 10 sec., then resume slowly.

Name: **Date:**

Target situation

Signs of a rising stress	Braking signal	Strategies for regaining self-control

Name: **Date:**

Target situation

Signs of a rising stress	Braking signal	Strategies for regaining self-control

Homework ⑭

ONE-STEP RELAXATION +
Coping with frustration

What is the goal?

> *To improve* your emergency braking techniques.
>
> *To learn* to recognize frustration as a signal for instituting coping strategies.

What do I have to do?

1. Practice one-step relaxation regularly.

2. Every time you feel frustrated, use coping strategies to regain self-control. Then plan to avoid repetition of same stress. (See example sheet.)

Name: Example sheet

Date:

Signs of frustration	Short-term coping	Long-term coping
I have an agenda planned for the meeting, but others prolong it to talk of other things. Feel impatient, start to interrupt them.	Say "stop." Reduce my physical tension and focus on what they are saying.	Attempt to get agreement before next meeting on length and agreement.
My wife and I repeat the same argument re home improvement costs: "She'll never understand."	Stop the discussion. "I'm too upset to discuss this rationally now. Can we do it tomorrow at 8 pm?"	Schedule planning session in which each expresses needs and fears and try to negotiate compromise on 1 or 2 specific points. Repeat as needed.
Son is late for swimming lesson. "He doesn't know the value of money and my time!"	Try to keep cool. Yelling won't make him move faster.	Set up situation where he pays for missed lesson from his allowance.
Supplier is late with promised shipment.	Grin and bear it.	Decide that the best I can do is grin and bear it.

Name: **Date:**

Signs of frustration	Short-term coping	Long-term coping

Name:		Date:
Signs of frustration	**Short-term coping**	**Long-term coping**

Homework ⑮

Creating a psychological balance sheet

What is the goal?

To learn to identify pleasant feelings and the situations that produce them.

To become aware of the balance of pleasures versus displeasures in our daily lives.

What do I have to do?

1. Every hour on the hour, note how you feel and classify the feeling as "pleasure" or "displeasure." Then note the acitivity.

2. At the end of each day, add up the number of pleasures versus displeasures. (See example sheet.)

Name: Example sheet				Date:

Time	Feelings	Pleasure	Displeasure	Activity
a.m. 7h:00	Boredom		X	Putting on makeup
8h:00	Interest, curiosity	X		Reading mail
9h:00	Challenge, apprehension	X		Preparing report for meeting
10h:00	Tension, frustration			Colleague challenges report
11h:00	Satisfied	X		Meeting over
12h:00	Hunger, good appetite	X		Time for lunch
p.m. 13h:00	Warmth, smiling	X		Walk in sunshine
14h:00	Anxiety		X	Rush job for yesterday!
15h:00	Concentration, working hard	X		Working on rush job
16h:00	Disappointed		X	Results not as good as wanted
17h:00	Rushed, irritable		X	Driving home
18h:00	Rushed, irritable		X	Preparing dinner
evening 19h:00	Enjoying food	X		Eating dinner
20h:00	Relaxed, content	X		Hot bath
21h:00	Excitement, enthusiasm	X		Watching TV
22h:00	Disgust, anger		X	Hockey player given unfair penalty
23h:00	Sleepy, tired	X		Go to bed
24h:00				
Total		10	6	

Name:				Date:

Time	Feelings	Pleasure	Displeasure	Activity
a.m. 7h:00				
8h:00				
9h:00				
10h:00				
11h:00				
12h:00				
p.m. 13h:00				
14h:00				
15h:00				
16h:00				
17h:00				
18h:00				
evening 19h:00				
20h:00				
21h:00				
22h:00				
23h:00				
24h:00				
Total				

Time	Feelings	Pleasure	Displeasure	Activity
a.m. 7h:00				
8h:00				
9h:00				
10h:00				
11h:00				
12h:00				
p.m. 13h:00				
14h:00				
15h:00				
16h:00				
17h:00				
18h:00				
evening 19h:00				
20h:00				
21h:00				
22h:00				
23h:00				
24h:00				
Total				

Name:　　　　　　　　　　**Date:**

Time	Feelings	Pleasure	Displeasure	Activity
a.m. 7h:00				
8h:00				
9h:00				
10h:00				
11h:00				
12h:00				
p.m. 13h:00				
14h:00				
15h:00				
16h:00				
17h:00				
18h:00				
evening 19h:00				
20h:00				
21h:00				
22h:00				
23h:00				
24h:00				
Total				

Name:

Date:

Homework ⑯

Creating a wish list

What is the goal?

To make a list of activities that give you pleasure.

What do I have to do?

1. Equip yourself with paper and pencil, and settle yourself in a quiet spot where you will be undisturbed.

2. Brainstorm activities that you have found pleasant in the past or that you think might give you pleasure. Do *not* judge the practicality of your wishes at this point; just list them. (See example sheet.)

Wish list of pleasurable activities

		P	F
1.	Take a month and travel around world.		
2.	Wish I spent more time playing with my children.		
3.	Time to just sit quietly and do nothing.		
4.	Get to see some hockey games.		
5.	Go out to a good restaurant for dinner.		
6.	Would really like to improve my swimming stroke.		
7.	Buy a boat and go sailing every weekend.		
8.	Spend more time in physical exercise.		
9.	More and better sex life!		
10.	Classify pictures I took during trip last summer.		
11.	Buy a new shirt.		

Wish list of pleasurable activities

	P	F
1.		
2.		
3.		
4.		
5.		
6.		
7.		
8.		
9.		
10.		
11.		

Homework  17

Making wishes happen

What is the goal?

To *develop* an action plan to increase pleasurable activity.

What do I have to do?

Follow action plan on next page.

Name: Example sheet	Date:

Step 1: Choosing a target wish

Consult your list of wishes. Choose *one* item that has a
favorable cost–benefit ratio.

Target wish: Get more exercise.

Step 2: List practical requirements to make this wish happen and how
to fulfill them.

Practical requirements | How to fulfill them

a. Decide what exercise, when, and where.

a. Get list of fitness classes from the local Y. Choose one and enroll.

b. Exercise clothes.

b. Buy jogging shoes next Saturday.

c. Physician's O.K.

c. Make appointment with medical dept.

d.

d.

e.

e.

Step 3:   Overcoming obstacles

List potential obstacles and how to overcome them.

Potential obstacles	How to overcome them
a. I may do too much at first, get hurt, and quit.	**a.** Exercise only in supervised class for beginners.
b. Other things might interfere with my schedule.	**b.** Choose a regular time most likely to be free — e.g., early morning before work or just after work.
c. My husband might object.	**c.** Explain what you want to do and ask for his help.
d. I have to miss classes because of travel.	**d.** Ask your instructor for a program to follow while traveling.
e. I don't like the YMCA.	**e.** Investigate company subsidies for other clubs.

Step 4:   *Express your goals* in concrete terms (e.g., *x* times per week).
Make sure they are realistic.

Goals:

Exercise 30 min., 3x per week.

Step 5: Starting date

I shall start my pleasurable activity on   Monday

Step 6: Recording progress

I shall record my progress by   ① Keeping a record of each class attended or exercise session done on my own.   ② Noting how much of the exercises in each class I can comfortably do — e.g., no. of minutes jogging.

Step 7: Evaluation

I shall evaluate my progress on   10 weeks after starting.

How do I feel?

How do I look?

Name:	Date:

Step 1: Choosing a target wish

Consult your list of wishes. Choose *one* item that has a favorable cost–benefit ratio.

Target wish:

Step 2: List practical requirements to make this wish happen and how to fulfill them.

Practical requirements

How to fulfill them

a. _____ a. _____

b. _____ b. _____

c. _____ c. _____

d. _____ d. _____

e. _____ e. _____

Step 3: Overcoming obstacles

List potential obstacles and how to overcome them.

Potential obstacles	How to overcome them
a. _____	a. _____
_____	_____
b. _____	b. _____
_____	_____
c. _____	c. _____
_____	_____
d. _____	d. _____
_____	_____
e. _____	e. _____
_____	_____

Step 4: *Express your goals* in concrete terms (e.g., *x* times per week). Make sure they are realistic.

Goals:

Step 5: Starting date

I shall start my pleasurable activity on

Step 6: Recording progress

I shall record my progress by

Step 7: Evaluation

I shall evaluate my progress on

Name:	Date:

Step 1: Choosing a target wish

Consult your list of wishes. Choose *one* item that has a
favorable cost–benefit ratio.

Target wish:

Step 2: List practical requirements to make this wish happen and how
to fulfill them.

Practical requirements   How to fulfill them

a. _____   a. _____
_____   _____

b. _____   b. _____
_____   _____

c. _____   c. _____
_____   _____

d. _____   d. _____
_____   _____

e. _____   e. _____
_____   _____

Step 3: Overcoming obstacles

List potential obstacles and how to overcome them.

Potential obstacles   How to overcome them

a. _____   a. _____

b. _____   b. _____

c. _____   c. _____

d. _____   d. _____

e. _____   e. _____

Step 4: *Express your goals* in concrete terms (e.g., *x* times per week).
Make sure they are realistic.

Goals:

Step 5:   Starting date

I shall start my pleasurable activity on

Step 6:   Recording progress

I shall record my progress by

Step 7:   Evaluation

I shall evaluate my progress on

Homework ⑱

Relapse prevention

What is the goal?

To learn to *anticipate* and *deal* with relapses in self-control.

What do I have to do?

1. *List a number* of danger situations that might cause *you* to *stop practicing* good stress management skills. These can be external (traveling) or internal (depressive period).

2. *For each danger* situation, think of *some warning signals* you can use to alert you that your stress management skills are slipping. These signs can be physical, mental, emotional, or behavioral.

3. For each danger situation, *indicate the remedial action* you can take to get on track again.

Name: Example sheet   **Date:**

	Potential danger situation	Potential warning signals	Remedial action
1.	Disruption of routine — e.g., going on a trip.	Slipping back to old ways: rushing, shouting.	① Reread section on braking signals. Use them.
2.	Period of heavy work pressure.	Arguments with colleagues.	① Increase relaxation practice. ② Examine self-talk. ③ Plan a pleasurable break as soon as possible.
3.			
4.	Family crisis	Feel tense and irritable. Headaches; trouble sleeping.	① Insofar as possible, use problem-solving techniques to deal with situation. ② Ask for emotional support from others.
5.			③ Use relaxation and productive thinking to reduce tension.

Name: Date:

	Potential danger situation	Potential warning signals	Remedial action
1.			
2.			
3.			
4.			
5.			

Name: **Date:**

	Potential danger situation	Potential warning signals	Remedial action
1.			
2.			
3.			
4.			
5.			